United States Government Accountability Office

Report to Congressional Requesters

I0425847

February 2012

WARFIGHTER SUPPORT

DOD Needs Strategic Outcome-Related Goals and Visibility over Its Counter-IED Efforts

G A O

Accountability ★ Integrity ★ Reliability

GAO-12-280

February 2012

WARFIGHTER SUPPORT

DOD Needs Strategic Outcome-Related Goals and Visibility over Its Counter-IED Efforts

Why GAO Did This Study

Over $18 billion has been appropriated to the Joint Improvised Explosive Device (IED) Defeat Organization (JIEDDO) to address the improvised explosive device (IED) threat, and there is widespread consensus that this threat will continue to be influential in future conflicts. DOD established the Joint Improvised Explosive Device Defeat Organization (JIEDDO) in 2006 to lead, advocate, and coordinate all DOD actions in support of the combatant commanders' and their respective joint task forces' efforts to defeat IEDs. This report, one in a series on JIEDDO's management and operations, addresses the extent to which DOD (1) has provided a comprehensive counter-IED strategic plan including measurable objectives that determine the effectiveness of efforts across DOD to combat IEDs, and (2) has identified counter-IED initiatives and activities, and coordinated these efforts. To address these objectives GAO reviewed counter-IED efforts from fiscal years 2006 through 2011, reviewed and analyzed relevant strategic-planning documents, collected and reviewed data identifying DOD counter-IED efforts, and met with DOD and service officials.

What GAO Recommends

GAO recommends four actions for DOD to develop a comprehensive strategic plan with strategic outcome-related goals and a complete listing of counter-IED efforts to maximize its resources. DOD concurred with one of the recommendations but did not concur with three. GAO continues to believe that its recommendations are warranted as discussed in the report.

View GAO-12-280. For more information, contact Cary B. Russell at (404) 679-1808 or russellc@gao.gov

What GAO Found

As the responsible DOD agency for leading, advocating, and coordinating all DOD efforts to defeat improvised explosive devices (IED) the Joint IED Defeat Organization (JIEDDO) was directed to develop DOD's counter-IED strategic plan in February 2006 under DOD Directive 2000.19E. As previously recommended by GAO, JIEDDO has made several attempts to develop such a plan, but its strategic-planning actions have not followed leading strategic-management practices or have since been discontinued. For example, JIEDDO's 2007 strategic plan did not contain a means of measuring its performance outcomes— a leading strategic-management practice. In addition, JIEDDO's 2009–2010 strategic plan contained performance measures, but JIEDDO discontinued using these measures because it later determined that the measures were not relevant to the organization's goals. Although DOD tasked JIEDDO to develop its counter-IED strategic plan, DOD has not translated DOD's counter-IED general mission objective of eliminating IEDs as a weapon of strategic influence into actionable goals and objectives. JIEDDO issued a new counter-IED strategic plan in January 2012; however, the new plan does not apply to all other counter-IED efforts departmentwide, only to those managed by JIEDDO. Consequently, JIEDDO's new strategic plan alone will not provide the means necessary for determining the effectiveness of all counter-IED efforts across DOD. Further, as JIEDDO implements its plan, it will continue to face difficulty measuring effectiveness until DOD establishes and provides results-oriented goals to accompany its general mission objective. Without actionable goals and objectives established by DOD, JIEDDO and other DOD components cannot tie individual performance measures to DOD's desired outcomes. As a result, DOD and external stakeholders will be left without a comprehensive, data-driven assessment as to whether their counter-IED efforts are achieving DOD's mission and will not be informed about the overall effectiveness of its counter-IED efforts or use of resources as they relate to DOD's mission.

DOD has not fully identified its counter-IED initiatives and activities, and as a result is not able to effectively coordinate these efforts across DOD. In attempting to develop a comprehensive database, as previously recommended by GAO, JIEDDO has used at least three systems to collect and record complete information on DOD's counter-IED efforts but discontinued each of them for reasons including lack of timeliness, comprehensiveness, or cost. For example, beginning in 2009, JIEDDO pursued Technology Matrix as a possible counter-IED database for all efforts within the DOD. However, JIEDDO discontinued support for Technology Matrix as a database since DOD did not require all relevant organizations to provide information to JIEDDO, and therefore it was not comprehensive. Without an automated means for comprehensively capturing data on all counter-IED efforts, the military services may be unaware of potential overlap, duplication, or fragmentation. For example, GAO identified six systems that DOD components developed to emit energy to neutralize IEDs, and DOD spent about $104 million collectively on these efforts, which could be duplicative because the military services did not collaborate on these efforts. Given the lack of a DOD-wide counter-IED database, other efforts may be overlapping.

_____ United States Government Accountability Office

Contents

Abbreviations

DOD	Department of Defense
IED	improvised explosive device
JIEDDO	Joint Improvised Explosive Device Defeat Organization
MRAP	Mine Resistant Ambush Protected
TAC	Tripwire Analytical Capability

This is a work of the U.S. government and is not subject to copyright protection in the United States. The published product may be reproduced and distributed in its entirety without further permission from GAO. However, because this work may contain copyrighted images or other material, permission from the copyright holder may be necessary if you wish to reproduce this material separately.

United States Government Accountability Office
Washington, DC 20548

February 22, 2012

The Honorable Adam Smith
Ranking Member
Committee on Armed Services
House of Representatives

The Honorable Roscoe G. Bartlett
Chairman
The Honorable Silvestre Reyes
Ranking Member
Subcommittee on Tactical Air and Land Forces
Committee on Armed Services
House of Representatives

Through fiscal year 2011, Congress has appropriated over $18 billion to the Joint Improvised Explosive Device Defeat Organization (JIEDDO) to address the improvised explosive device (IED) threat.[1] In addition, other Department of Defense (DOD) components, including the military services, have spent billions of dollars from their own funds developing counter-IED capabilities. For example, the Mine Resistant Ambush Protected (MRAP) Task Force, which leads DOD's efforts to produce and field MRAP vehicles to protect troops against IEDs and other threats, received over $40 billion from fiscal years 2005 through 2010. The IED threat continues to be a major concern in Afghanistan in addition to other areas throughout the globe, with over 500 IED events per month worldwide outside of Southwest Asia, according to JIEDDO. There is widespread consensus that this threat will not go away and that IEDs will continue to be a weapon of strategic influence in future conflicts. In fighting the IED threat, both JIEDDO and the services have taken steps to reduce IED incidents and casualties. For example, during 2010, JIEDDO

---

[1] This total represents appropriations and rescissions made to the Joint Improvised Explosive Device Defeat Fund for JIEDDO. Generally, these funds are available for the purpose of allowing the Director of JIEDDO "to investigate, develop and provide equipment, supplies, services, training, facilities, personnel and funds" to assist U.S. forces in IED defeat. *See, e.g.,* Department of Defense and Full-Year Continuing Appropriations Act, 2011, Pub. L. No.112-10, div. A, tit. IV (2011). The appropriation provisions often specify that the Secretary of Defense may transfer funds to other appropriations categories to accomplish this purpose after notifying the congressional defense committees. *See id.*

initiated 49 major efforts, which according to JIEDDO, made significant contributions toward defeating the IED threat.

Prior to the establishment of JIEDDO in 2006, no single entity was responsible for coordinating the DOD's counter-IED efforts. DOD established JIEDDO and directed it to lead, advocate, and coordinate all DOD actions in support of the combatant commanders and their respective joint task forces' efforts to defeat IEDs as weapons of strategic influence.[2] DOD's directive mandates that JIEDDO's director serve as the DOD point of coordination for initiatives across the full range of efforts necessary to defeat the IED threat, integrate all counter-IED solutions throughout DOD, and coordinate with other DOD components for ongoing midterm research and development initiatives and long-term science and technology efforts, among other duties.[3] A primary role for JIEDDO is to provide funding and assistance to rapidly develop, acquire, and field counter-IED solutions.

In response to direction from congressional committees,[4] we have reported on several issues related to JIEDDO's management and operations. Specifically, in a March 2007 classified report, we reported on JIEDDO's lack of a strategic plan and the resulting effects on the development of its financial and human capital management programs. We made several recommendations based on this finding to the Secretary of Defense to improve the management of JIEDDO operations, stressing the need for JIEDDO to develop a detailed strategic plan that would clearly articulate JIEDDO's mission and the types of counter-IED solutions it should provide and include results-oriented goals and objectives and measures of success. In addition, we testified and issued

---

[2] *Department of Defense Directive 2000.19E,* Joint Improvised Explosive Device Defeat Organization (JIEDDO) ¶ 4 (Feb. 14, 2006) (hereinafter cited as DODD 2000.19E (Feb. 14, 2006)); Memorandum from the Deputy Secretary of Defense, Establishment of the Joint Improvised Explosive Device Defeat Organization (JIEDDO) (Jan. 18, 2006). DODD 2000.19E superseded DODD 2000.19, Joint Improvised Explosive Device (IED) Defeat (June 27, 2005), and facilitated the transformation of the IED Defeat entity from a joint task force into a joint organization.

[3] *See* DODD 2000.19E, ¶ 6.2 (Feb. 14, 2006).

[4] *See, e.g.,* H.R. Rep. No. 110-477, at 1003-04 (2007) (conference report accompanying the National Defense Authorization Act for Fiscal Year 2008); S. Rep. No. 109-292, at 239-40 (2006) (report of the Senate Committee on Appropriations, accompanying the Department of Defense Appropriations Bill, 2007).

a report in October 2009, in which we noted that despite the creation of JIEDDO, many of the organizations engaged in the counter-IED effort prior to JIEDDO continued to develop, maintain, and expand their own counter-IED capabilities.[5] In July 2010, we reported that JIEDDO did not have metrics that inform DOD about the effect of the agency's efforts on combating IEDs as a weapon of strategic influence.[6] Accordingly, you requested that we assess the progress DOD and JIEDDO have made with regard to counter-IED strategic planning and achieving comprehensive visibility over DOD-wide counter-IED activities. Specifically, this review addresses the extent to which (1) DOD has provided a comprehensive counter-IED strategic plan including results-oriented strategic goals and performance metrics to determine the effectiveness of efforts across DOD to combat IEDs, and (2) DOD has identified counter-IED initiatives and activities, and coordinated these efforts.

To address these objectives, we considered DOD counter-IED efforts from fiscal years 2006 through 2011. To analyze the extent to which DOD has provided a comprehensive counter-IED strategic plan including strategic results-oriented goals and metrics that determine the effectiveness of efforts across DOD to combat IEDs, we reviewed DOD's counter-IED strategic-planning documents that we gathered from JIEDDO as well as the Combatant Commands. In addition, we also interviewed JIEDDO officials involved in strategic planning and assessment to learn about the implementation of the actions detailed in some of the documents. From these documents and interviews, we identified several triggering actions that either provided the impetus for, or resulted in, strategic management efforts. We compared these actions against leading strategic management practices and principles demonstrated by

---

[5] GAO, Warfighter Support: *Actions Needed to Improve Visibility and Coordination of DOD's Counter-Improvised Explosive Device Efforts*, GAO 10-95 (Washington D.C., Oct. 29, 2009); GAO Warfighter Support: *Challenges Confronting DOD's Ability to Coordinate and Oversee Its Counter-Improvised Explosive Devices Efforts*, GAO-10-186T, (Washington D.C. Oct. 29, 2009).

[6] GAO, Warfighter Support: *Actions Needed to Improve the Joint Improvised Explosive Device Defeat Organization's System of Internal Control*, GAO-10-660 (Washington D.C., Jul.1, 2010).

successful results-oriented organizations[7] and rated each according to their fulfillment of these leading practices. To determine the extent to which DOD has identified counter-IED initiatives and activities, and coordinated these efforts, we reviewed JIEDDO databases on counter-IED efforts and interviewed DOD, Service, and JIEDDO officials to determine the degree of comprehensive awareness regarding DOD's counter-IED efforts.

We conducted this performance audit between June 2010 and February 2012 in accordance with generally accepted government auditing standards. Those standards require that we plan and perform the audit to obtain sufficient, appropriate evidence to provide a reasonable basis for our findings and conclusions based on our audit objectives. Appendix I contains additional details of our scope and methodology.

Background

Created by the Deputy Secretary of Defense in January 2006, JIEDDO is responsible for leading, advocating, and coordinating all DOD actions in support of the combatant commanders' and their respective joint task forces' efforts to defeat IEDs as weapons of strategic influence. Prior DOD efforts to defeat IEDs included various process teams and task forces. For example, DOD established the Joint IED Defeat Task Force in June 2005 for which the Army provided primary administrative support. This task force replaced the Army IED Task Force, the Joint IED Task Force, and the Under Secretary of Defense, Force Protection Working Group. To focus all of DOD's efforts and minimize duplication, DOD published a new counter-IED policy in February 2006 through DOD Directive 2000.19E, which changed the name of the Joint IED Defeat Task Force to JIEDDO and established it as a joint entity and jointly

---

[7] GAO, Highlights of a GAO Forum: *Mergers and Transformation: Lessons Learned for a Department of Homeland Security and Other Federal Agencies* GAO-03-293SP (Washington D.C.: Nov. 14, 2002), GAO, Transportation Security Administration: *Actions and Plans to Build a Results-Oriented Culture* GAO-03-190 (Washington D.C.: Jan. 17, 2003), GAO, Results-Oriented Cultures: *Implementation Steps to Assist Mergers and Organizational Transformations* GAO-03-669 (Washington D.C.: Jul. 2, 2003), GAO, Defense Business Transformation: *Achieving Success Requires a Chief Management Officer to Provide Focus and Sustained Leadership* GAO-07-1072 (Washington D.C.: Sep. 5, 2007), GAO, Unmanned Aircraft Systems: *Additional Actions Needed to Improve Management and Integration of DOD Efforts to Support Warfighter Needs* GAO-09-175 (Washington D.C.: Nov. 14, 2008), GAO, Unmanned Aircraft Systems: *Comprehensive Planning and a Results-Oriented Training Strategy Are Needed to Support Growing Inventories* GAO-10-331 (Washington D.C.: Mar. 26, 2010)

staffed organization within DOD, reporting directly to the Deputy Secretary of Defense.[8] The directive states that JIEDDO shall "focus" (i.e., lead, advocate, and coordinate) all DOD actions in support of the Combatant Commanders' and their respective Joint Task Forces' efforts to defeat IEDs as "weapons of strategic influence."[9]

In prior GAO reviews, we reported on several issues related to JIEDDO's management and operations. In March 2007, we reported JIEDDO's lack of a strategic plan and the resulting effects on the development of its financial and human capital management programs. We made several recommendations based on this finding to the Secretary of Defense to improve the management of JIEDDO operations, stressing the development of JIEDDO's detailed strategic plan. Subsequently, we also reported in March 2008 on JIEDDO's internal controls and made several recommendations focused at improving JIEDDO's internal control system.[10] JIEDDO agreed with our recommendations and undertook efforts to address our findings and recommended actions. In addition, we testified and issued a report in October 2009 regarding steps that JIEDDO and DOD have taken to manage counter-IED efforts.[11] Our testimony also included some of the challenges we later discussed in a report released in July 2010 about JIEDDO's lack of effective output performance measures,[12] internal control weaknesses, and the lack of adherence to its approval process for counter-IED initiatives. We made several recommendations to JIEDDO focused on improving its internal

---

[8] *See* DODD 2000.19E, ¶¶ 1.2, 5, 7.1.1 (Feb. 14, 2006). The issuance of the Directive followed a January 2006 memo from the Deputy Secretary of Defense announcing the establishment and mission of JIEDDO. *See* Memorandum from the Deputy Secretary of Defense, Establishment of the Joint Improvised Explosive Device Defeat Organization (JIEDDO) (Jan. 18, 2006).

[9] *See* DODD 2000.19E, ¶ 4 (Feb. 14, 2006).

[10] GAO, Defense Management: *More Transparency Needed over the Financial and Human Capital Operations of the Joint Improvised Explosive Device Defeat Organization*, GAO-08-342 (Washington D.C.: Mar. 6, 2008).

[11] GAO-10-95; GAO-10-186T.

[12] In the context of performance plans and similar provisions found in certain sections of Title 31 of the U.S. Code, output measures are defined as the tabulation, calculation, or recording of activity or effort that can be expressed in a quantitative or qualitative manner; outcome measures are an assessment of the results of a program activity compared to its intended purpose. *See* 31 U.S.C. § 1115(h)(7), (8).

controls. DOD and JIEDDO agreed with our recommendations and have taken actions in response.

DOD Has Not Provided a Results-Oriented Strategic Plan to Manage Its Counter-IED Efforts

Beginning in February 2006, JIEDDO has been responsible for developing DOD's IED defeat strategic plan for countering the IED threat,[13] but its strategic-planning actions have not followed leading strategic management practices, or have since been discontinued. In March 2007, we found that JIEDDO had not developed a strategic plan and as a result could not assess whether it was making the right investment decisions or whether it had effectively organized itself to meet its mission. We recommended that the Secretary of Defense require the Director of JIEDDO, in developing DOD's IED defeat strategic plan, to clearly articulate JIEDDO's mission and specify goals, objectives, and measures of effectiveness. JIEDDO fully concurred with our recommendations and was working to complete a strategic plan when we issued this report, and in September 2007, JIEDDO completed its DOD-wide counter-IED strategic plan. However, JIEDDO's 2007 strategic plan did not contain a means of measuring its performance outcomes, which is a leading strategic management practice. Subsequent JIEDDO strategic-planning efforts also did not follow leading strategic management practices or have been discontinued. For example, JIEDDO's 2009–2010 strategic plan contained performance measures, but JIEDDO discontinued using these measures because they determined that the data from these measures were not relevant to the organization's goals. We have previously reported that good strategic planning helps organizations (1) make the key decisions that will drive their actions, (2) measure the effectiveness of their actions to achieve intended results, and (3) if not achieving intended results, have the data to determine modifications needed to achieve intended results—all attributes of a plan that helps maximize organizational resources.[14] Many of JIEDDO's plans contained output measures such as the percentage of initiatives for which JIEDDO completes operational assessments or the percentage of counter-IED initiatives that were adopted by one of the Military Services. While collecting outputs is an important initial step in measuring progress,

---

[13] See DODD 2000.19E, ¶ 6.2.9 (Feb. 14, 2006). Specifically, JIEDDO is to coordinate with the DOD components to develop, publish, and update this plan.

[14] GAO-03-293SP; GAO-03-190; GAO-03-669; GAO-07-1072; GAO-09-175; GAO-10-331.

they do not provide information about progress toward achieving JIEDDO's mission as outcome measures would.

Since 2006, JIEDDO has made several attempts to develop a counter-IED strategic plan including its 2007 and 2009–2010 strategic plans, which in the case of the 2007 plan, included elements for guiding DOD subordinate organizations and the military services involved with counter-IEDs in developing their own counter-IED planning. However, those plans did not have outcome-related goals specific enough for JIEDDO and these organizations to be able to develop enduring measures of effectiveness that inform DOD whether its counter-IED mission is being met. As shown in figure 1, we identified 17 key actions or triggering events applicable to DOD that were to either produce counter-IED strategic plans for the department or further develop the strategic plans. However, the 17 actions have either been discontinued or did not satisfy key strategic-management-planning practices, including developing results-oriented strategic goals, performance measures, and the adjustment of plans or intended actions based on the results of these measures.[15] For some of the 17 actions and events, we found that while JIEDDO had made efforts to satisfy leading strategic management practices, these efforts fell short of developing results-oriented goals and performance measures that link with DOD's counter-IED mission. We assessed some efforts as partially fulfilling strategic management practices because developing output measures is a step toward developing outcome measures, and measuring individual initiatives contributes toward the overall counter-IED effort. However, JIEDDO has not expanded its assessments beyond these individual efforts and determined how these efforts, overall, help to achieve DOD's counter-IED mission.

---

[15] Some of these best practices are discussed in GAO, *Executive Guide: Effectively Implementing the Government Performance and Results Act*, GGD-96-118, (Washington, DC: June 1, 1996). The report discussed principles and practices demonstrated by results-oriented organizations.

Figure 1: Instances of Incomplete or Insufficient Counter-IED Strategic Management from 2006 to 2011

Interactivity instructions: Roll over the bull's-eye next to the event to view more information

First JIEDDO Director

2006

February 2006 — ● DOD Defined JIEDDO's Mission and Directed it to Develop a Strategic Plan
  0 1 2 3 4

● GAO Recommended JIEDDO Develop a Strategic Plan
  0 1 2 3 4

● Congressional Committee Directed DOD to Finalize JIEDDO's Strategic Plan
  0 1 2 3 4

● DOD Issued DOD-wide C-IED Strategic Plan
  0 1 2 3 4

March 2007

2007

● JIEDDO Wrote in its 2007 Annual Report that it had Issued an Implementation Instruction for Its Strategic Plan
  N/A
  0 1 2 3 4

September 2007 — ● C-IED Conference Recommended Development of Metrics
  0 1 2 3 4

December 2007 — ● JIEDDO Established Metrics in its Organization and Functions Guide
January 2008   0 1 2 3 4

Change in Director

2008

● Strategy for FYs 2009 Through 2010 Created
  0 1 2 3 4

● C-IED Conference Recommended Development of Metrics
  0 1 2 3 4

December 2008 — ● JIEDDO Began to Establish Initiative Evaluation Plans Early in Initiative Development
February 2009   0 1 2 3 4

March 2009 — ● JIEDDO Wrote a C-IED Strategic Management Paper
  0 1 2 3 4

2009

● GAO Recommended JIEDDO Improve Process for Assessing Effectiveness
  0 1 2 3 4

● JIEDDO Drafted Overarching Assessment Processes and Procedures Manual
  0 1 2 3 4

Change in Director

● 2011 JIEDDO Execution Plan Created
  0 1 2 3 4

April 2010
May 2010
2010
July 2010

● C-IED Conference Recommended the Development of a Standardized Assessment Framework
  0 1 2 3 4

● JIEDDO Drafted C-IED Strategy to Coincide with Draft DOD Directive Revision
  N/A
  0 1 2 3 4

December 2010

February 2011 — ● JIEDDO to Revise its Draft C-IED Strategy to Incorporate Anticipated New National C-IED Policy Requirements[a]
March 2011   N/A
  0 1 2 3 4

Change in Director

July 2011

2011

September 2011

Degree of follow-through or completion of leading strategic management practices[b]

▒ Fulfills leading management practice

▨ Partially fulfills leading management practice[c]

Develop a mission statement — 0 ↑ 1 Develop results-oriented strategic goals ↑ 2 Develop performance measures ↑ 3 ↑ 4 Apply acquired knowledge to improve performance

Source: GAO analysis.

[a]JIEDDO issued its 2012-2016 Counter-IED Strategic Plan in early January 2012 and issued the detailed performance measurements annex on January 19, 2012. However, because JIEDDO's plan was competed subsequent to our review, we did not evaluate the plan's compliance with leading strategic management practices. Moreover, JIEDDO's plan is limited as a strategic plan for DOD's counter-IED efforts because it has not been adopted as DOD's department-wide strategic plan for managing all of its counter-IED expenditures and investments made by military services and DOD agencies other than JIEDDO.

[b]Criteria used to rank the instances were taken from GAO Executive Guide: Effectively Implementing the Government Performance and Results Act GGD-96-118, (Washington DC, Jun 1, 1996).

[c]In these examples, JIEDDO created strategic goals or developed a means of measuring performance; however in these cases the goals were not results-oriented or the performance measurements were not linked to strategic goals or were discontinued. Thus, we give partial credit for developing goals and measures but not full credit for fulfilling leading strategic management practices.

GAO-12-280 Warfighter Support

In early January 2012, JIEDDO issued its counter-IED strategic plan for 2012–2016, which established five principal goals for JIEDDO with three to six supporting objectives for each goal. This plan did not specify what actions JIEDDO planned to take to achieve these goals. On January 19, 2012, JIEDDO augmented its strategic plan by issuing an annex detailing numerous actions to achieve these objectives, and establishing 230 separate metrics that JIEDDO expects will provide the means of assessing its progress. In addition, JIEDDO is planning to begin, in March 2012, quarterly internal reviews to assess progress and make adjustments to its counter-IED efforts accordingly. Such action has not been a step JIEDDO has included in its past efforts. We see good potential in JIEDDO's strategic plan; however, because the portion of the plan relevant to our recommendations was issued on January 19, 2012—shortly before issuance of this report—we did not evaluate the plan and have not therefore assessed the extent to which this new plan will follow leading strategic management practices and provide results-oriented strategic goals and sufficient performance metrics for JIEDDO. Further, according to JIEDDO officials, the strategic plan applies only to counter-IED efforts managed by JIEDDO and does not apply to all other counter-IED efforts departmentwide. Consequently, successful implementation of JIEDDO's strategic plan alone will not provide the means necessary for determining the effectiveness of all counter-IED efforts across DOD. According to JIEDDO officials, DOD will produce a departmentwide counter-IED strategic plan in the future, but there is no specified timeline for issuance of this plan.

As JIEDDO moves forward to implement its counter-IED strategic plan, and DOD develops a departmentwide counter-IED strategic plan, DOD will continue to face difficulty in developing measures of effectiveness, if it does not have results-oriented strategic goals to accompany DOD's general counter-IED mission statement. The department has identified eliminating IEDs as a weapon of strategic influence as the overarching mission of its counter-IED programs, but has not translated this mission into actionable goals and objectives. Without actionable goals and objectives established by DOD, JIEDDO, and other DOD components cannot tie individual performance measures to DOD's desired outcomes. As a result, DOD and external stakeholders are left without a comprehensive, data-driven assessment as to whether DOD's counter-IED efforts are achieving DOD's mission. Furthermore, without a means to measure the success of JIEDDO's efforts in achieving DOD's counter-IED mission, JIEDDO's basis for determining how to invest its resources among its three lines of organizational effort—to attack the network, defeat the device, and train the force—is limited. While JIEDDO has established procedures to assess counter-IED gaps and prioritize and manage its requirements and individual investments—including coordinating and collaborating with various DOD entities—to rapidly pursue these critical lines of effort,[16] JIEDDO and DOD are not informed about the overall effectiveness of their counter-IED efforts and use of resources as they relate to DOD's mission.

Lastly, JIEDDO has not had a completed, fully developed strategic plan until recently, with long-term strategic goals that informed incoming directors about which actions have taken place and which must be continued in order to maintain continuous progress toward achieving long-term goals. Having such a strategic plan would have benefitted JIEDDO leadership as JIEDDO's directors changed four times over the 6 years JIEDDO has existed (see fig. 1). Without this framework, new strategic-planning efforts have been initiated under each of these directors to improve the organization and manage counter-IED support—efforts that contributed in varying degrees to strategic management but, as discussed above, were not implemented or were discontinued in many instances. Now that JIEDDO has completed its strategic plan, it should work to ensure that implementation helps provide continuity for the organization as JIEDDO leadership changes in the future.

---

[16] According to its Director, JIEDDO coordinates its counter-IED initiatives with numerous DOD offices, including the Under Secretary of Defense for Acquisition Technology and Logistics, the Under Secretary of Defense—(Comptroller), J3 and J8 from the Joint Staff, and the Military Services.

DOD Has Some Visibility over Counter-IED Initiatives but Does Not Have a Comprehensive Listing of All DOD Counter-IED Initiatives

DOD does not have full visibility over all of its counter-IED efforts. DOD relies on various sources and systems for managing its counter-IED efforts, but has not developed a process that provides DOD with a comprehensive listing of its counter-IED initiatives and activities. For example, JIEDDO has developed the JIEDDO Enterprise Management System to manage its own operations by collecting and reporting cost and other information related to JIEDDO's organizational and funds management, its coordination of JIEDDO funded projects and projects funded by other DOD activities, its administrative activities, and its own counter-IED projects.[17] However, while this system contains information that could be used to identify individual initiatives, it does not automatically separate costs directly expended on counter-IED initiatives from JIEDDO's infrastructure and overhead costs such as facilities, contractor services, pay and benefits, and travel. Consequently, this system does not provide an automated means to comprehensively and rapidly identify and list all of JIEDDO's counter-IED initiatives. Further, even if it did collect this information, the system is limited to JIEDDO, and therefore would not include a comprehensive listing of other DOD efforts outside of JIEDDO. However, JIEDDO is required by DOD Directive to lead, advocate, and coordinate all DOD actions in support of combatant commanders' and their respective joint task forces' efforts to defeat IEDs as weapons of strategic influence.[18] In 2008, a congressional subcommittee noted the absence of any indication that DOD processed (e.g., synthesized or kept a database) or made use of information it received regarding DOD-wide counter-IED activities.[19] Further, in October 2009, we recommended that the Secretary of Defense direct the military services to work with JIEDDO to develop a database for all DOD counter-IED initiatives. DOD concurred and stated that several counter-IED databases have been established across DOD.[20] However, DOD has not yet fully implemented this recommendation. While DOD has used various

---

[17] JEMS is the umbrella system for all of JIEDDO's information IT systems and as such we are using it to represent JIEDDO's information technology systems collectively without listing its various sub-systems.

[18] See DODD 2000.19E, ¶ 4 (Feb. 14, 2006).

[19] See Subcommittee on Oversight & Investigations of the House Armed Services Committee, 110th Cong., *The Joint Improvised Explosive Device Defeat Organization: DOD's Fight Against IEDs Today and Tomorrow* (Comm. Print No. 110-11, November 2008).

[20] GAO-10-95.

systems over time as listed below, to collect and record complete information on its counter-IED efforts, it has discontinued each of them for this purpose. DOD therefore still lacks a database for listing all DOD counter-IED initiatives. As a result, DOD may not be able to effectively coordinate counter-IED efforts across DOD, including JIEDDO, the military services, and relevant DOD agencies.[21]

- Quarterly Congressional Report Appendix: Beginning in 2008, JIEDDO listed all DOD counter-IED initiatives in its quarterly IED report to Congress to provide Congress with insight into DOD's counter-IED initiatives and activities. In 2009, JIEDDO reduced this listing to a subset of DOD's counter-IED initiatives. However, according to JIEDDO officials, JIEDDO increased interactions with congressional staff to improve transparency into DOD's counter-IED initiatives and activities. According to JIEDDO officials, the information discussed in these meetings provided congressional staff with key information that was more current than that provided by the quarterly reports. According to JIEDDO officials, in 2010, congressional staff from the Senate and House Armed Services Committees indicated to JIEDDO that they no longer needed to receive quarterly reports. JIEDDO discontinued issuance of the quarterly report and ceased collecting listings of counter-IED efforts from the department as a whole.[22] JIEDDO continues to meet with congressional staff to discuss key counter-IED efforts, but without the benefit of a

---

[21] Recently, a provision in the Ike Skelton National Defense Authorization Act for Fiscal Year 2011 required DOD to develop and maintain "a comprehensive database" with information for coordinating, tracking, and archiving each counter-IED initiative within DOD. See Pub. L. No. 111-383, § 124(a)(1) (2011). Among other purposes, DOD is to use the information to identify and eliminate redundant initiatives. See § 124(a)(2)(A). DOD is also required to develop appropriate means to measure the effectiveness of these initiatives and to prioritize funding accordingly. See § 124(b).

[22] A provision in the National Defense Authorization Act for Fiscal Year 2012 repealed certain quarterly reporting requirements. See Pub. L. No. 112-81, § 1062(d)(5) (2011). However, reporting requirements for other information related to counter IED efforts may remain.

comprehensive list of counter-IED efforts that would provide a better basis for determining key efforts to report to Congress.[23]

- Technology Matrix Database: In 2009, DOD developed this database through JIEDDO in response to our recommendation to establish a comprehensive counter-IED database, expending a total of $225,000.[24] JIEDDO requested sponsorship from DOD Deputy Director for Research and Engineering to make this database an official repository of DOD technology information for counter-IED efforts, and require full participation of all DOD entities. However, the database was not fully developed in its concept, structure, and procedures. Thus, the Research and Engineering officials did not require all organizations involved in developing counter-IED solutions to use this database until these shortcomings were addressed. Without this requirement from Research and Engineering, JIEDDO concluded that the database could not provide comprehensive counter-IED information as intended, and JIEDDO discontinued using this database for this purpose in early 2010 and looked to other ongoing alternatives to provide this capability.

- Tripwire Analytical Capability (TAC): JIEDDO acquired and further developed this system in 2009 for intelligence querying purposes but also explored this system for possible use in collecting comprehensive data on DOD's counter-IED initiatives managed by the military services and other DOD agencies outside of JIEDDO, automatically through programmed computer interfaces. JIEDDO considered using this data to populate a JIEDDO counter-IED database. However, according to JIEDDO officials, JIEDDO subsequently determined that less expensive commercially available alternatives were available and discontinued its exploration of TAC in May 2011 for collecting DOD counter-IED data. At the time JIEDDO ceased considering TAC for

---

[23] In a report accompanying the Department of Defense Appropriations Bill for fiscal year 2012, the Senate Committee on Appropriations directed JIEDDO to submit to congressional defense committees monthly commitment, obligation, and expenditure data by line of operation—defeat the device, attack the network, train the force, and staff and infrastructure—and by year of appropriation. Additionally, the Committee directed JIEDDO to submit to the congressional defense committees monthly reports of obligation data on a project-by-project basis by line of operation. See S. Rep. No. 112-77, at 275 (2011). However, if this direction is applied only to JIEDDO-funded projects, the reports may not capture DOD-funded counter-IED projects outside of those funded by JIEDDO.

[24] GAO-10-95

use in collecting data on DOD's counter-IED initiatives, JIEDDO had not expended any additional funds on TAC specifically for this purpose.[25]

JIEDDO is currently developing a new JIEDDO-wide information technology architecture and plans to develop a database for counter-IED efforts across DOD as part of this new architecture. This effort is in the conceptualization stage, and JIEDDO officials do not anticipate completion before the end of fiscal year 2012. Further JIEDDO does not have an implementation plan that includes a detailed timeline with milestones, a key management practice, to help track its progress in achieving this goal.[26]

Faced with the current absence of a DOD-wide counter-IED listing, which we had previously recommended JIEDDO develop, JIEDDO developed a master list of its own internally-funded, active counter-IED initiatives in May 2011. Because JIEDDO does not have an automated mechanism that reliably and quickly identifies its own counter-IED initiatives, JIEDDO must review its system for collecting and managing its funds used in order to identify, differentiate, and determine which of its funded activities are stand-alone counter-IED initiatives and which are administrative and indirect overhead activities. JIEDDO's funds-tracking system contained 887 unique identification numbers assigned from 2006 to May 2010 to categorize and manage its expenditures. According to JIEDDO officials, review of its funds management system has been labor intensive and is not yet completed because the funds management system does not contain an automated mechanism or coding to differentiate between all expenditures for administrative and indirect overhead versus expenditures for stand-alone counter-IED initiatives.[27] For example, in December 2010, JIEDDO established a requirement for the review of its active counter-IED initiatives by JIEDDO stakeholders in preparation for certain major milestone decisions and meetings. However, JIEDDO did not have an automated mechanism to identify its stand-alone counter-IED

---

[25] All funds expended by JIEDDO for TAC were directly related to intelligence querying purposes.

[26] GAO-09-175.

[27] JIEDDO's expenditure tracking system, does not differentiate between expenditures it makes that constitute overhead and infrastructure and expenditures it makes that JIEDDO considers to be separate, stand alone counter-IED initiatives.

initiatives, and therefore, when JIEDDO began implementation of this process in May 2011, it had to review one by one its 887 funds tracking system numbers to separate its stand-alone counter-IED initiatives from overhead. JIEDDO completed this review June 17, 2011, and concluded that 223, or approximately 25 percent, of JIEDDO's 887 expenditure-tracking-system control numbers were currently active stand-alone counter-IED initiatives.[28] While this list could provide JIEDDO and external stakeholders with a comprehensive inventory of active JIEDDO-funded counter-IED initiatives, it is incomplete because it does not identify or separate out inactive stand-alone counter-IED initiatives from administrative overhead expenditures. According to JIEDDO officials, JIEDDO could produce a comprehensive list of its counter-IED initiatives in a matter of 2 to 4 days, but had not done so as of December 15, 2011. Further, if JIEDDO did produce such a list, it would represent one point in time and would not provide a comprehensive DOD-wide database of counter-IED efforts because it would not include counter-IED efforts funded and managed by other DOD components independently of JIEDDO.

Without a comprehensive listing of counter-IED initiatives, DOD components may be unaware of the total spectrum of counter-IED efforts within the department, and thereby continue to independently pursue counter-IED efforts that focus on similar technologies and may be duplicative. In our March 2011 report[29] and ongoing work, we identified several instances of potential duplication, overlap, and fragmentation within DOD regarding its counter-IED efforts by analyzing overlap in the capabilities and function of these systems. The following are examples we identified:

- Counter-IED Directed Energy Technology: The military services have developed six different systems that emit energy, such as radio waves, directed at IEDs to neutralize them.[30] While detailed data

---

[28] According to JIEDDO, active initiatives are those with ongoing JIEDDO funding commitments from JIEDDO, or those that JIEDDO has not terminated or transferred to other DOD entities for management.

[29] GAO, *Opportunities to Reduce Potential Duplication in Government Programs, Save Tax Dollars, and Enhance Revenue* GAO-11-318SP (Washington D.C.: Mar. 1, 2011).

[30] The systems are being developed by the Air Force, Army, Navy and Marine Corps with some funding provided by JIEDDO.

available on the six initiatives are classified, the efforts exhibit a range of different approaches regarding physical size, weight, and cost, and data show that the various DOD components involved have spent about $104 million collectively on these efforts to date. However, given the lack of a DOD-wide counter-IED database, there could be more directed energy efforts that we have not identified. Moreover, concerns regarding the fragmentation and duplication in DOD's directed energy counter-IED efforts have risen to the highest levels within the warfighter community. Specifically, the commander of U.S. Central Command, in August 2011, conveyed concern regarding issues including apparent "duplicity of [development] effort" in directed energy technology with organizations (in DOD) working different solutions. The correspondence called for coordination and cooperation by DOD on its directed energy efforts to develop a directed energy system that works in theater as quickly as possible given that the development has been under way since 2008. In response, in August 2011, JIEDDO, as DOD's coordinating agency for these efforts, developed a plan and, in September 2011, brought various service program offices together to develop a solution as soon as possible. According to JIEDDO officials, the six systems will continue in development through fiscal year 2012, at which point, JIEDDO will determine which of the systems best satisfies U.S. Central Command's requirement. While this new approach may eliminate future unnecessary duplication of effort, earlier coordination and better visibility could have prevented duplication that may have occurred up to this point. According to JIEDDO officials, the level of concern expressed and the fact that the concern was expressed in writing resulted in JIEDDO being able to secure the cooperation needed by the various organizations working different directed energy solutions to coordinate in this instance. However, this is a unique occurrence because, according to JIEDDO officials, JIEDDO does not have the authority to direct—i.e., compel— various DOD organizations that may be working on overlapping technologies or efforts to reach consensus regarding selection among competing alternatives. Therefore, JIEDDO has not always been successful in securing the cooperation of the services to coordinate on counter-IED efforts.

- Radio Frequency Jamming Systems: The Army and Navy continue to pursue separate developments of counter-IED jamming systems, which provide a limited radius of protection to prevent IEDs from being triggered by an enemy's radio signals. In 2007, DOD established the Navy as single manager and executive agent for ground-based jamming.[31] Under DOD Directive 5101.14, military services may conduct ground-based jammer research and development to satisfy military service-unique requirements if the requirements are coordinated before initiation with the DOD's single manager for jammers and, for any system or system modifications resulting from such efforts, operational technical characteristics and logistics plans are approved by the single manager.[32] The Navy has developed a standard technology and system for ground-based jamming called JCREW I1B1,[33] which DOD has designated as the ground-based jamming program for the entire Department. However, the Army has continued to develop its own ground-based jamming system called Duke. According to Navy officials, in 2010, the Army continued to develop new technology for insertion into its Duke system—expected to cost about $1.062 billion when completed and installed—without notifying and coordinating with the Navy as DOD's single manager for ground-based jammer technology. According to Army officials, the Army is pursuing development of its own system because it intends to expand the use of this technology for purposes other than countering IEDs such as jamming enemy command, control, and communication systems. However, according to Navy officials, the CREW system's technology has the flexibility and capacity to expand and provide the same additional functions as the Army plans for its Duke system. Moreover, according to Navy officials, the Navy's system is further along in its development. Because the Navy and Army are pursuing separate jamming systems, it is not clear if DOD is taking the most cost-effective approach. While, according to JIEDDO officials, the Office of Secretary of Defense was considering how to resolve this issue, a decision had not been made before this report was completed. Regardless of the final outcome however, a more

---

[31] The Secretary of the Navy, as the Executive Agent for Military Ground-Based CREW Technology, is responsible for designating a flag grade officer as the single manager for CREW. *See* Department of Defense Directive 5101.14, DoD Executive Agent and Single Manager for Military Ground-Based Counter Radio-Controlled Improvised Explosive Device Electronic Warfare (CREW) Technology, ¶ 5.3.1 (June 11, 2007) (hereinafter cited as DODD 5101.14 (June 11, 2007)).

[32] *See* DODD 5101.14, ¶ 4 (June 11, 2007).

[33] JCREW is used to abbreviate "Joint Counter Radio-Controlled Improvised Explosive Device Electronic Warfare"

coordinated approach early in the process when initiating programs of this magnitude could prevent unnecessary duplication in costs and effort. [34]

- Electronic Data Collection Systems: According to JIEDDO officials, JIEDDO has funded the development and support of approximately 70 electronic data collection and analysis tools that overlap to some degree because they include capabilities to collect, analyze, and store data to help the warfighter combat the IED threat. Although JIEDDO recently reported that it could not verify total funding for its information technology investments,[35] GAO determined through a review of DOD financial records that DOD has expended at least $184 million collectively on information technology development for its data collection and analysis tools. According to JIEDDO officials, JIEDDO is aware of the redundancy within these electronic tools. In April 2011, the JIEDDO Deputy Director for Information Management raised the issue of redundancy in JIEDDO's information technology systems including its counter-IED data collection and analysis systems and tools. Consequently, since April 2011, JIEDDO has worked to eliminate overlapping information-technology capabilities where feasible including among the approximately 70 analytical tools JIEDDO has funded and developed for use in countering IED networks. For example, on July 1, 2011, JIEDDO discontinued funding for one of these initiatives—Tripwire Analytical Capability (TAC)—citing as reasons TAC's limited purpose, high cost, and duplicative capabilities. However, in making the decision to discontinue TAC yet continue operating the other data collection and analysis tools, JIEDDO had not compared and quantified all of the potential options to streamline or consolidate these tools to create a single collective system that includes extracting data on counter-IED efforts across DOD. As a result, JIEDDO cannot be certain it is

---

[34] The Senate Appropriations Committee recently noted the Navy's executive agent and single manager role for CREW, as well as a DOD Inspector General report documenting a disconnect between the Army and DOD CREW programs. The Committee recommended denying funds requested by the Army for fiscal year 2012 to initiate an Integrated Electronic Warfare Systems program, stating that the Committee did "not believe it is prudent to initiate a new program of this magnitude that has such significant overlap with the Department's program of record." See S. Rep. No. 112-77, at 174-75 (2011).

[35] REPORT OF AUDIT 2011-07-002: Joint Improvised Explosive Device Defeat Organization: Information Technology Investment Management, *Joint Improvised Explosive Device Defeat Organization Office of Internal Review*, 6 September 2011.

pursuing the most advantageous approach for collecting, analyzing, storing, and using available data for combating the IED threat. Further, although JIEDDO has discontinued funding TAC, the Defense Intelligence Agency is continuing to develop the tool for its own use, resulting in the potential for DOD-wide duplication between TAC and JIEDDO's other data collection and analysis tools.

Conclusions

Six years after DOD established JIEDDO as its coordinating agency to lead, advocate, and coordinate responses to the IED threat across the department, DOD continues to lack comprehensive visibility of its counter-IED expenditures and investments, including those from JIEDDO, the military services, and relevant DOD agencies. The absence of a strategic plan with outcome-oriented goals and visibility over DOD's counter-IED efforts are recurring themes that we have identified in prior reports as affecting JIEDDO's ability to manage DOD's efforts effectively and efficiently. JIEDDO has demonstrated progress in addressing previously raised issues—by developing a formal, more rigorous internal control system, and in issuing a 2012–2016 strategic plan for the management of JIEDDO's counter-IED efforts—but these actions have not fully addressed the issues we have raised in this report. Specifically, DOD has not implemented adequate actions to (1) provide a comprehensive plan to ensure that all DOD counter-IED efforts are strategically managed in order to achieve its goal to defeat IEDs as a weapon of strategic influence, and (2) comprehensively list all DOD-wide counter-IED initiatives in a database that provides internal and external parties with visibility into the department's counter-IED efforts. Without a comprehensive plan and listing of its counter-IED initiatives, DOD continues to risk fragmentation, overlap, and duplication in its counter-IED efforts, such as those identified in this report, as well as lack the ability to prioritize projects within future budget levels. Given the limited applicability of JIEDDO's recently issued strategic plan and the limited progress JIEDDO has made in implementing our prior recommendation regarding developing a comprehensive listing of DOD-wide efforts, it is critical that DOD places greater focus and emphasis on the actions it takes in addressing these issues. As the nation addresses fiscal challenges, and DOD is directed to identify efficiencies, it will need to reduce and eliminate unnecessary duplicative counter-IED initiatives. We therefore reiterate our prior recommendation that the Secretary of Defense direct the military services to work with JIEDDO to develop a database for all DOD's counter-IED initiatives.

Recommendations for Executive Action

In addition to the prior recommendation reiterated above that remains open, we recommend that the Secretary of Defense direct the Deputy Secretary of Defense, who is responsible for direction and control of JIEDDO, to take the following four actions:

- Define outcome-related strategic goals associated with DOD's counter-IED mission to enable the development of measures of effectiveness that will help to determine progress of DOD's counter-IED efforts.
- Assess JIEDDO's recently completed strategic plan and its implementation to ensure that it
  - incorporates outcome-related strategic goals,
  - includes sufficient measures of effectiveness to gauge progress, and
  - uses the data collected from these metrics to adjust its counter-IED efforts, as needed.
- Develop an implementation plan for the establishment of DOD's counter- IED database including a detailed timeline with milestones to help achieve this goal.
- Develop a process to use DOD's counter-IED database once it is established to identify and compare all counter-IED initiatives and activities, to enable program monitoring, and reduce any duplication, overlap, and fragmentation among counter-IED initiatives.

Agency Comments and Our Evaluation

In written comments on a draft of this report, DOD concurred with the third of our four recommendations—to develop an implementation plan for the establishment of DOD's counter-IED database—and did not concur with the other three. DOD's written comments are included in appendix II. DOD also provided technical comments that we have incorporated into this report where appropriate.

In disagreeing with our first recommendation for the Deputy Secretary of Defense to define outcome-related strategic goals associated with DOD's counter-IED mission to enable the development of measures of effectiveness that will help to determine progress of DOD's counter-IED efforts, the department stated that the JIEDDO Director has accomplished this task by issuing its 2012–2016 counter-IED strategic plan in January 2012. While we agree that the recent issuance of JIEDDO's plan is a positive development, it does not fully address our recommendation because the plan does not apply to all counter-IED efforts departmentwide. According to JIEDDO officials, the plan applies to the management of JIEDDO counter-IED efforts only and has not been adopted as DOD's strategic plan for managing all of its counter-IED expenditures and investments from the military services and relevant DOD agencies. Therefore, JIEDDO's strategic goals do not satisfy the need for the Deputy Secretary of Defense to define outcome-related strategic goals for the department taken as a whole, and we believe our recommendation remains valid.

In disagreeing with our second recommendation for the Deputy Secretary of Defense to document and assess JIEDDO's strategic plan to ensure that it incorporates outcome-related strategic goals, includes sufficient measures of effectiveness to gauge progress, and uses the data collected from these metrics to adjust its counter-IED efforts, as needed, the department stated that JIEDDO has established outcome-related strategic goals and measures of effectiveness in its January 2012 strategic plan and related implementation plan. DOD further stated that in March 2012 JIEDDO will begin quarterly internal reviews to assess progress against its goals and make adjustments to its counter-IED efforts. Completion of JIEDDO's strategic plan is a positive step; however, because the portion of the plan relevant to our prior recommendations— the annex containing measures of effectiveness, timelines, and goals— was issued on January 19, 2012, we were unable to evaluate the plan before issuance of this report and therefore cannot comment on its adequacy relative to our recommendations. However, JIEDDO's numerous prior strategic-planning actions have not followed leading strategic management practices, or have been discontinued. Therefore, JIEDDO's recently completed counter-IED strategic plan and plans for internal quarterly reviews alone do not negate the need for the Deputy Secretary of Defense to assess the adequacy of JIEDDO's strategic plan and its implementation, and we believe our recommendation remains valid. However, we modified the language in our recommendation to reflect the fact that JIEDDO has now recently issued a strategic plan and to clarify that the remaining action needed by the Deputy Secretary of Defense is to assess its adequacy and implementation.

In concurring with our third recommendation for the Deputy Secretary of Defense to develop an implementation plan for the establishment of DOD's counter- IED database, DOD stated that DOD Directive 2000.19E is currently being revised to create a requirement for Combatant Commands, military services, and DOD agencies to report counter-IED initiatives to JIEDDO. According to DOD, this step will enable JIEDDO to develop a database for all DOD counter-IED initiatives. We agree that establishing this requirement should help JIEDDO's counter-IED database development; however, according to JIEDDO officials, DOD Directive 2000.19E has been under revision for 2 years without DOD issuing a new directive. Therefore, it is critical that DOD complete this task as soon as possible to enable JIEDDO to develop its planned counter-IED database as described in DOD's comments.

In disagreeing with our fourth recommendation for the Deputy Secretary of Defense to develop a means to identify and reduce any duplication, overlap, and fragmentation among counter-IED initiatives, DOD stated that it had existing processes and organizations including JIEDDO and its Senior Integration Group to facilitate coordination and collaboration with the military services and across DOD, which would address this recommendation. We agree that existing DOD processes such as JIEDDO's Capabilities Development Process and DOD's Senior Integration Group prioritization process can be helpful in coordinating DOD's counter-IED efforts. However, the effectiveness of DOD's existing coordination and collaboration processes has been limited given that these processes did not prevent the issues of potential duplication we identified in this report. For example, in the case of DOD's directed energy counter-IED efforts where DOD has collectively expended $104 million, the processes cited by DOD in its response did not identify and resolve the fragmentation and potential duplication present in these efforts. As a result, the commander of U.S. Central Command, as mentioned previously, protested in writing to DOD officials about potential duplication of efforts. Without an adequate process to use DOD's counter-IED database, once it is developed, DOD will continue to lack assurance that it is identifying and addressing instances of potential duplication before making significant investments. In finalizing our report, we modified the wording of our recommendation to clarify our intent that DOD establish a process (rather than a means) to use its counter-IED database once it is established.

In addition to comments on our recommendations, DOD questioned the accuracy of our statements regarding the soundness of JIEDDO's prioritization and resource allocation determinations. Specifically, DOD stated that our report was inaccurate in stating that JIEDDO does not have a sound basis to determine how to invest DOD's resources among the lines of operation: attack the network, defeat the device, and train the force. DOD further stated that JIEDDO has established procedures to assess counter-IED gaps and prioritize requirements in coordination with warfighting commanders and that JIEDDO coordinates counter-IED initiatives with numerous DOD offices, which DOD concluded ensures warfighting priorities, effectiveness of fielded counter-IED efforts, and cost reasonableness are addressed and evaluated. DOD also asserted that JIEDDO's existing programming and prioritization processes align

JIEDDO's investment resources with Combatant Commander priorities. We recognize that JIEDDO has resource allocation and prioritization processes in place and have modified the language of this report to acknowledge these processes where applicable. However, we maintain our position that JIEDDO's basis for determination of resource allocations and prioritizations is limited because DOD has not been able to identify all of its counter-IED efforts, as stated above, and lacks actionable goals and objectives needed to tie JIEDDO's and the Department's performance measures to outcomes that would assess its counter-IED efforts. Therefore, DOD does not have full assurance that its investments are achieving its strategic goal in the counter-IED fight.

We are sending copies of this report to other interested congressional committees and the Secretary of Defense. In addition, this report will be available at no charge on the GAO Web site at http://www.gao.gov.

If you have any questions regarding this report, please contact me at (404) 679-1808 or at russellc@gao.gov. Contact points for our Offices of Congressional Relations and Public Affairs may be found on the last page of this report. Key contributors are listed in appendix IV.

Cary B. Russell, Acting Director
Defense Capabilities and Management

Appendix I: Scope and Methodology

We considered counter-IED strategic planning efforts from February 2006 through 2012. To analyze the extent to which DOD has provided a comprehensive counter-IED strategic plan including strategic results-oriented goals and metrics that determine the effectiveness of efforts across DOD to combat IEDs, we collected and reviewed DOD's counter-IED strategic-planning documents from JIEDDO. We also reviewed prior GAO reports and work papers involving strategic planning and management, both for JIEDDO and for the government in general. We used these GAO reports to identify leading strategic management practices derived from leading strategic management principles demonstrated by successful results-oriented organizations for use as evaluation criteria in this review. In addition, we interviewed JIEDDO officials involved in strategic planning and assessment to learn about the implementation of the actions detailed in the counter-IED strategic planning documents collected. Furthermore, we attended a counter-IED conference sponsored by JIEDDO in March 2011 that focused on a key element of strategic planning and management—measuring outcomes and performance—to observe and collect additional information relevant to DOD's counter-IED strategic management. From the documents collected and interviews conducted, we identified several triggering actions that either provided the impetus for, or resulted in, counter-IED strategic management efforts in JIEDDO or elsewhere in DOD. We compared these actions against leading strategic management criteria described above and rated each according to its fulfillment of these leading practices.

We considered counter-IED efforts from fiscal years 2006 through 2011 managed by DOD components with involvement in counter-IED efforts: JIEDDO, military services, combatant commands, and defense agencies. To determine the extent to which DOD has identified counter-IED initiatives and activities, and coordinated these efforts, we reviewed JIEDDO databases on counter-IED efforts and interviewed OSD, military service and JIEDDO officials to discuss the availability of data about additional counter-IED efforts/initiatives. Through our interactions with JIEDDO officials, we determined that the best, most comprehensive repository of counter-IED information that currently existed was the Technology Matrix. We analyzed the Technology Matrix to obtain a list of persons, for each organization, who had entered information regarding counter-IED efforts into the database. Additionally, we reviewed and analyzed prior GAO counter-IED work to obtain relevant contact information, obtained current contact information of relevant organizations through our Inspector General liaison, and reviewed and analyzed other external sources of information, which contained relevant organizations.

We interviewed OSD, Service, and JIEDDO officials to discuss and determine awareness of DOD's counter-IED efforts. To determine the effects of the absence of a comprehensive DOD listing of counter-IED initiatives within the department, we assessed whether DOD components continue to independently pursue counter-IED efforts that may be redundant or overlapping. We updated counter-IED initiatives case studies that we previously reported as having redundancy of effort and developed additional case studies of overlapping counter-IED efforts within DOD. We purposefully selected the additional case studies based on information in interviews with DOD officials or in data or documentation collected during this review that evidenced similar capabilities and objectives among two or more counter-IED efforts. In each case study, we compared the overlapping counter-IED efforts to determine and describe the degree of redundancy and potential duplication among the efforts for each case study given overlap of the capabilities and functions of these systems.

Appendix II: Supplemental Table to Figure 1

The following table identifies 17 key actions or triggering events applicable to DOD that were to either produce counter-IED strategic plans for the department or further develop the strategic plans. This table is similar to figure 1 but shows the interactive text without needing the interactive computer capability.

Table 1: Instances of Incomplete or Insufficient Counter-IED Strategic Management from 2006 to 2011

Date	Event	Details Related to Event
February 2006	DOD Defined JIEDDO's Mission and Directed it to Develop a Strategic Plan	DOD provided JIEDDO with the counter-IED mission to "defeat [IEDs] as weapons of strategic influence," but DOD did not provide results-oriented strategic goals on which to base a strategic plan.
March 2007	GAO Recommended JIEDDO Develop a Strategic Plan	JIEDDO concurred with our recommendations.
March 2007 and September 2007	Congressional Committee Directed DOD to Finalize JIEDDO's Strategic Plan	A congressional committee directed DOD in March and September 2007 to finalize and submit JIEDDO's strategic plan. JIEDDO produced a document in September 2007 that contained a mission statement but did not include results-oriented strategic goals or performance measures.
September 2007	DOD Issued DOD-wide C-IED Strategic Plan	This 9-page DOD-wide plan clarified the mission of JIEDDO and contained strategic goals. However, these goals were not results-oriented, and the plan did not include performance measures.
December 2007	JIEDDO Wrote in its 2007 Annual Report that it had Issued an Implementation Instruction for Its Strategic Plan	As of February 17, 2012, JIEDDO was unable to locate the implementation instruction, and therefore could not provide a description of the instruction's purpose or contents.
January 2008	C-IED Conference Recommended Development of Metrics	JIEDDO produced metrics and collected data subsequent to this recommendation; however, according to JIEDDO, the collection of data for these metrics was discontinued by 2009.
December 2008	JIEDDO Established Metrics in its Organization and Functions Guide	JIEDDO created metrics in this guide, but they were not representative of JIEDDO's work and were never implemented according to JIEDDO. JIEDDO's 2011 Organization and Functions Guide stated that measures of effectiveness are under development and will be updated in future publications, but none had been published as of February 17, 2012.
February 2009	Strategy for FYs 2009 Through 2010 Created	Plan contained strategic goals and proposed performance measures; however, the performance measures were later abandoned because they were not relevant to the work performed by JIEDDO staff.
March 2009	C-IED Conference Recommended Development of Metrics	According to JIEDDO, the measurements that it developed were related to outputs, not outcomes, and thus were limited in assessing performance.
April 2010	JIEDDO Began to Establish Initiative Evaluation Plans Early in Initiative Development.	As of February 17, 2012, JIEDDO had created evaluation plans for 24 of its 32 initiatives started after April 2010. The plans designated tests, evaluations, and data to be collected to determine the level of performance regarding these initiatives.
May 2010	JIEDDO Wrote a C-IED Strategic Management Paper	JIEDDO wrote a C-IED strategic paper, but DOD did not adopt it as an official strategic document with implementation authority. Further, the paper contained ideas gathered from within JIEDDO on C-IED goals but because they were not results-oriented, the paper lacked specifications for developing results-oriented metrics.

Date	Event	Details Related to Event
July 2010	GAO Recommended JIEDDO Improve Process for Assessing Effectiveness	JIEDDO concurred with our recommendation and produced an Assessment Methodology which was to provide a consistent approach for evaluating initiatives individually, and was not intended to link with results-oriented strategic goals.
December 2010	JIEDDO Drafted Overarching Assessment Processes and Procedures Manual	Draft manual described the process for conducting assessments and tied together different assessment areas but was never finalized and, as of February 17, 2012, JIEDDO had not issued an assessment manual that was results-oriented.
February 2011	2011 JIEDDO Execution Plan Created	The Execution Plan, linking its activities to budget priorities over a 2-year period, enabled JIEDDO to prioritize its initiatives' funding decisions. However, the plan focused on tactical, short-term decisions and did not contain long-term strategic goals or a framework for assessing progress toward meeting goals.
March 2011	C-IED Conference Recommended the Development of a Standardized Assessment Framework	JIEDDO continued to meet periodically with a working group formed at the March 2011 C-IED Conference to develop measures of effectiveness as part of an assessment framework. However, as of February 17, 2012, JIEDDO had not published a final assessment framework to enable it to measure performance.
July 2011	JIEDDO Drafted C-IED Strategy to Coincide with Draft DOD Directive Revision	JIEDDO drafted a strategic plan based on anticipated changes in DOD Directive 2000.19E. However, the departing Deputy Secretary of Defense did not approve the revised directive.
September 2011	JIEDDO to Revise its Draft C-IED Strategy to Incorporate Anticipated New National C-IED Policy Requirements	JIEDDO officials stated that their strategy will incorporate requirements from a forthcoming national C-IED policy as well as the revised DOD Directive 2000.19E. Once DOD approves the scheduled revision of 2000.19E, JIEDDO officials said they plan to issue a C-IED strategy containing results-oriented strategic goals and action plans containing related metrics. JIEDDO officials also said they plan to adjust action plans based on the resulting data from these metrics. As of February 17, 2012, neither the national policy nor the revised DOD directive had been issued.

Source: GAO analysis.

Appendix III: Comments from the Department of Defense

JOINT IED DEFEAT ORGANIZATION
5000 ARMY PENTAGON
WASHINGTON DC 20310-5000

JAN 2 7 2012

Mr. Cary Russell
Acting Director, Defense Management and Capabilities
U.S. Government Accountability Office
441 G Street, NW
Washington, DC 20548

Dear Mr. Russell:

This is the Department of Defense (DoD) response to the GAO draft report, GAO-12-280, "WARFIGHTER SUPPORT: DOD Needs Strategic Outcome-Related Goals and Visibility over its Counter-IED Efforts" dated 12 January, 2012 (GAO Code 351526).

JIEDDO published its Counter-IED Strategy 2012 - 2016 effective 1 January 2012, as noted in your report. It provides strategic goals with associated objectives. Those goals were broadly written to allow for institutional, DoD, Service, and interagency support to the five enduring capabilities which are the foundation of the C-IED strategy. Implementation of the strategy is effected through Annex A, a supporting action plan, also published in January 2012. This action plan details the goals and objectives and provides supporting measureable outcomes (Measures of Effectiveness) and outputs (Measures of Performance).

The DoD Directive that established JIEDDO, *DODD 2000.19e, Joint Improvised Explosive Device Defeat Organization, February 2006,* is under revision and scheduled for update in early 2012. The revised DoDD 2000.19e will enable JIEDDO to implement the strategy and also the recommendations from GAO.

The essence of JIEDDO's rapid acquisition process is in placing a CIED capability into the hands of the warfighter as soon as practical. JIEDDO invests in multiple research and development initiatives (some within the same capability area) to increase the probability of rapidly delivering effective C-IED enablers to the warfighter. This entails using parallel paths to develop technologies and to mitigate risk. JIEDDO's organizational value is based on this ability and flexibility to satisfy Combatant Commanders (COCOM) urgent needs expeditiously by accepting a higher level of program risk. While accepting higher risk in rapidly providing capability to the warfighter, we cannot sacrifice effective stewardship of resources.

The Joint Improvised Explosive Device Defeat (JIEDD) Capability Approval and Acquisition Management Process (JCAAMP) ensures initiatives are vetted with Services, COCOMs, and DoD Agencies. It provides visibility of ongoing efforts within DoD such that JIEDDO makes informed decisions on whether to invest in parallel efforts to ensure urgently required C-IED capability are delivered expeditiously. The Senior Integration Group (SIG), chaired by the Deputy Secretary of Defense, provides overall review and oversight of all DoD C-IED initiatives.

Your report is inaccurate in stating that JIEDDO does not have a sound basis to determine how to invest our resources among the lines of operation: Attack the Network, Defeat the Device, and Train the Force. JIEDDO has established procedures to assess C-IED gaps and prioritize requirements (in coordination with warfighting commanders). JIEDDO coordinates C-IED initiatives with numerous DoD offices, including USD-AT&L, USD-Comptroller, J3 and J8 from the Joint Staff, and the Services. This coordination and collaboration ensures warfighting priorities, effectiveness of fielded C-IED enablers (resourced by JIEDDO or other DoD activities), and cost reasonableness are addressed and evaluated. JIEDDO develops a comprehensive investment plan to support our budget submissions, which is briefed and approved within DoD and Congress.

The enclosed attachment contains a detailed response to each recommendation. Comments on technical or factual corrections to the report were provided in a separate document to the GAO audit team. The point of contact for this response is Mr. William Rigby, JIEDDO Internal Review, william.rigby@jieddo.dod.mil, 703-602-4807.

Sincerely,

MICHAEL D. BARBERO
Lieutenant General, USA
Director

Enclosure:
As stated

2

Unclassified

**GAO DRAFT REPORT – DATED JANUARY 12, 2012,
GAO-12-280 (GAO CODE 351526)**

**"WARFIGHTER SUPPORT: DOD NEEDS STRATEGIC OUTCOME-RELATED
GOALS AND VISIBILITY OVER ITS COUNTER-IED EFFORTS"**

**DEPARTMENT OF DEFENSE COMMENTS
TO THE RECOMMENDATIONS**

RECOMMENDATION 1: The GAO recommends that the Secretary of Defense
through the Deputy Secretary of Defense direct the Director of the Joint Improvised
Explosive Device Defeat Organization (JIEDDO) to define outcome-related strategic
goals associated with DoD's counter-IED mission to enable the development of measures
of effectiveness that will help to determine progress of DoD's counter-IED efforts.

DOD RESPONSE: DoD non-concurs with the recommendation. As reflected in the
GAO's report, the JIEDDO Director has accomplished this task by issuing its Counter-
IED Strategic Plan (CSP) for 2012-2016 in early January 2012, which contains a
description of the threat as well as JIEDDO's capabilities, and JIEDDO's goals and
objectives. JIEDDO released the implementation plan (Annex A, Action Plan) soon after
the base document in mid-January 2012. It which includes measures of effectiveness and
provides a means for assessing progress against the defined actions to achieve JIEDDO's
strategic goals. Additionally, JIEDDO will begin quarterly internal reviews in March
2012 to assess progress and make adjustments to its counter-IED efforts.

RECOMMENDATION 2: The GAO recommends that the Secretary of Defense
through the Deputy Secretary of Defense direct the Director of the Joint Improvised
Explosive Device Defeat Organization (JIEDDO) to document and assess JIEDDO's
strategic plan to ensure that it: incorporates outcome-related strategic goals; includes
sufficient measures of effectiveness to gauge progress; and uses the data collected from
these metrics to adjust its counter-IED efforts, as needed.

DOD RESPONSE: DoD non-concurs with the recommendation. See response above.
JIEDDO has established outcome-related strategic goals and measures of effectiveness in
its C-IED Strategic Plan and Annex A, Action Plan. GAO's statement that "JIEDDO
does not have a sound basis to determine how to invest its resources among its three lines
of organizational effort" is inaccurate and fails to acknowledge JIEDDO's programming
and prioritization of resources in support of the warfighter. JIEDDO aligns resources
along the operation lines of Attack the Network, Defeat the Device, and Train the Force
based upon Combatant Commander's (COCOM) priorities.

Unclassified

Unclassified

RECOMMENDATION 3: The GAO recommends that the Secretary of Defense through the Deputy Secretary of Defense direct the Director of the Joint Improvised Explosive Device Defeat Organization (JIEDDO) to develop an implementation plan for the establishment of DOD's counter-IED database including a detailed timeline with milestones to help achieve this goal.

DOD RESPONSE: DoD concurs with the recommendation. DoDD 2000.19e, the directive establishing JIEDDO, is currently being staffed for revision. A specified task in this revision will require the COCOMs, Services and DoD agencies to report C-IED initiatives to JIEDDO. This revision will enable JIEDDO visibility of all C-IED initiatives, programming, and funding pursued on a unilateral basis by a Service, COCOM, or other DoD Component. The JIEDDO Enterprise Management System (JEMS) is JIEDDO's System of Record for hosting all C-IED initiative data.

RECOMMENDATION 4: The GAO recommends that the Secretary of Defense through the Deputy Secretary of Defense direct the Director of the Joint Improvised Explosive Device Defeat Organization (JIEDDO) to develop a means to identify and compare all counter-IED initiatives and activities, to enable program monitoring, and reduce any duplication, overlap, and fragmentation among counter-IED initiatives.

DOD RESPONSE: DoD non-concurs with the recommendation. JIEDDO and DoD's existing processes facilitate coordination and collaboration with the Services and across the DoD, which reduces duplication, overlap, and fragmentation with counter-IED initiatives. Through JIEDDO's Capabilities Development Process (JCDP), JIEDDO coordinates with all C-IED stakeholders and agencies with C-IED and related missions to determine required capabilities to address IED threats. Additionally, the Joint Improvised Explosive Device Defeat (JIEDD) Capability Approval and Acquisition Management Process (JCAAMP) uses a series of boards and governance bodies, such as the JORAB and JR2AB, which require participation from the Services and J8, to monitor C-IED programs across DoD and identify and address duplication and potential overlap. The Secretary of Defense also established the Senior Integration Group (SIG) and appointed JIEDDO's Director as the Secretariat of this group. Through serving as DoD's single authority to prioritize solutions that can be fielded quickly and to direct actions to resolve issues associated with joint urgent needs, the SIG ensures collaboration on C-IED initiatives across the DoD.

2

Unclassified

Appendix IV: GAO Contact and Staff Acknowledgments

GAO Contact	Cary Russell, (404) 679-1808 or russellc@gao.gov
Staff Acknowledgments	In addition to the contact named above, key contributors to this report were Grace Coleman, Rajiv D'Cruz, Emily Norman, Michael Shaughnessy, Rebecca Shea, Michael Silver, Amie Steele, William M. Solis, John Strong, and Tristan T.To.

Related GAO Products

Opportunities to Reduce Potential Duplication in Government Programs, Save Tax Dollars, and Enhance Revenue. GAO-11-318SP. Washington D.C.: March 1, 2011.

Warfighter Support: DOD's Urgent Needs Processes Need a More Comprehensive Approach and Evaluation for Potential Consolidation. GAO-11-273. Washington D.C.: March 1, 2011.

Warfighter Support: Actions Needed to Improve the Joint Improvised Explosive Device Defeat Organization's System of Internal Control. GAO-10-660. Washington D.C.: July 1, 2010.

Warfighter Support: Improvements to DOD's Urgent Needs Processes Would Enhance Oversight and Expedite Efforts to Meet Critical Warfighter Needs. GAO-10-460. Washington D.C.: April 30, 2010.

Unmanned Aircraft Systems: Comprehensive Planning and a Results-Oriented Training Strategy Are Needed to Support Growing Inventories. GAO-10-331. Washington D.C.: March 26, 2010.

Warfighter Support: Challenges Confronting DOD's Ability to Coordinate and Oversee Its Counter-Improvised Explosive Devices Efforts. GAO-10-186T. Washington D.C.: October 29, 2009.

Warfighter Support: Actions Needed to Improve Visibility and Coordination of DOD's Counter-Improvised Explosive Device Efforts. GAO-10-95. Washington D.C.: October 29, 2009.

Unmanned Aircraft Systems: Additional Actions Needed to Improve Management and Integration of DOD Efforts to Support Warfighter Needs. GAO-09-175. Washington D.C.: November 14, 2008.

Defense Management: More Transparency Needed over the Financial and Human Capital Operations of the Joint Improvised Explosive Device Defeat Organization. GAO-08-342. Washington D.C.: March 6, 2008.

Defense Business Transformation: Achieving Success Requires a Chief Management Officer to Provide Focus and Sustained Leadership. GAO-07-1072. Washington D.C.: September 5, 2007.

Results-Oriented Cultures: Implementation Steps to Assist Mergers and Organizational Transformations. GAO-03-669. Washington D.C.: July 2, 2003.

Transportation Security Administration: Actions and Plans to Build a Results-Oriented Culture. GAO-03-190. Washington D.C.: January 17, 2003.

Highlights of a GAO Forum: Mergers and Transformation: Lessons Learned for a Department of Homeland Security and Other Federal Agencies. GAO-03-293SP. Washington D.C.: November 14, 2002.

Executive Guide: Effectively Implementing the Government Performance and Results Act. GGD-96-118. Washington, D.C.: June 1, 1996.

GAO's Mission	The Government Accountability Office, the audit, evaluation, and investigative arm of Congress, exists to support Congress in meeting its constitutional responsibilities and to help improve the performance and accountability of the federal government for the American people. GAO examines the use of public funds; evaluates federal programs and policies; and provides analyses, recommendations, and other assistance to help Congress make informed oversight, policy, and funding decisions. GAO's commitment to good government is reflected in its core values of accountability, integrity, and reliability.
Obtaining Copies of GAO Reports and Testimony	The fastest and easiest way to obtain copies of GAO documents at no cost is through GAO's website (www.gao.gov). Each weekday afternoon, GAO posts on its website newly released reports, testimony, and correspondence. To have GAO e-mail you a list of newly posted products, go to www.gao.gov and select "E-mail Updates."
Order by Phone	The price of each GAO publication reflects GAO's actual cost of production and distribution and depends on the number of pages in the publication and whether the publication is printed in color or black and white. Pricing and ordering information is posted on GAO's website, http://www.gao.gov/ordering.htm. Place orders by calling (202) 512-6000, toll free (866) 801-7077, or TDD (202) 512-2537. Orders may be paid for using American Express, Discover Card, MasterCard, Visa, check, or money order. Call for additional information.
Connect with GAO	Connect with GAO on Facebook, Flickr, Twitter, and YouTube. Subscribe to our RSS Feeds or E-mail Updates. Listen to our Podcasts. Visit GAO on the web at www.gao.gov.
To Report Fraud, Waste, and Abuse in Federal Programs	Contact: Website: www.gao.gov/fraudnet/fraudnet.htm E-mail: fraudnet@gao.gov Automated answering system: (800) 424-5454 or (202) 512-7470
Congressional Relations	Katherine Siggerud, Managing Director, siggerudk@gao.gov, (202) 512-4400, U.S. Government Accountability Office, 441 G Street NW, Room 7125, Washington, DC 20548
Public Affairs	Chuck Young, Managing Director, youngc1@gao.gov, (202) 512-4800 U.S. Government Accountability Office, 441 G Street NW, Room 7149 Washington, DC 20548

Please Print on Recycled Paper.

www.ingramcontent.com/pod-product-compliance
Lightning Source LLC
Chambersburg PA
CBHW080932290526
45795CB00007BA/2727